LIFE WITH POLAR BEARS

A Children's book of colors and questions

*The first book with a heart beat or should
I say beats from the streets*

Written by Chad Elness

authorHOUSE®

AuthorHouse™
1663 Liberty Drive
Bloomington, IN 47403
www.authorhouse.com
Phone: 1-800-839-8640

First published by AuthorHouse   11/11/2011

ISBN: 978-1-4678-7407-6 (sc)
ISBN: 978-1-4678-7406-9 (ebk)

Library of Congress Control Number: 2011960734

Printed in the United States of America

Dedicated to all those who told me to turn it down,
My families and to Sweet Sarah

After each letter draw a picture that comes to you

Right, never wrong, at the end, you will be able to sing your song

Have fun, even when there is no sun

There is always someone shining on you, even when you're feeling a little blue

At the end of this book, I would like for you to take a look

At the world we see you and me, joining hands to become one

A love, so strong, once again you can never be wrong

Apple A day

A.

What's your favorite fruit?

Basketball

B.

What's your favorite sport?

Colors

C.

My favorite color is blue

How about you?

Does it matter?

D.

What things do you love?

Who do you love?

Everyday

E.

What things do you do everyday?

Fun with Family

F.

What do you like to do for fun?

Greatness

G.

What makes people great?

What makes you great?

Healthy Happy Heart

H.

How does one heal a heart that is not so happy?

Ice

I.

What makes ice so cool?

(sometimes when I'm hot
I jump in the pool)

Jack "the great" Johnson

Jump like Jordan

J.

Do you have a favorite song or a favorite number?

Kindness

K.

Where does it come from?

Love for Lisa (my sister)

L.

What is Love?
(love never fails)

Minneapolis, Minnesota M.

What is your hometown?

What makes it so special?

Names and Games
N.

Your name comes from who? What games do you play?

Oceans

O.

Oceans are so wonderful,
What makes them so
awesome?

Protection

P.

What does it mean to protect something?

Queen

Q.

What is your favorite card?

Respect the word respect R.

Is the word respect a word or a feeling? Who do you respect?

Sweet Sarah S.

What makes a person so special and sweet?

Trust

T.

Why is trust a must?

Unique

U.

What makes you so unique?

Virginia

V.

What is your favorite state?

Washington

W.

Which Washington do you like?

X. (my generation)

What would you change?
Would you rather have
some in your pocket?

Youth

Y.

How do we stay forever young? (Bob Dylan)

Zebras at the Zoo

Z.

How do we save the one and only Polar Bear?

Write your song, Sing your song..... with one big smile

After your done, grab someone's hand and walk a mile

The End